By the same author

Life's Meaning Journal

Dynamic Cognition – The DC Effect in Your Life

The Power of Caring and Your Field of Perception

LIFE S MEANING FOR TODAY

Steven Warren

Second Edition

First published in Great Britain in 2010
by Steven Warren Publishing

This paperback second edition published in 2012

A CIP catalogue record for this book is available from the British Library.

ISBN 978-1-908587-01-5

www.StevenWarrenPublishing.com

For more books, recordings and other materials by Steven Warren visit

www.StevenWarren.co.uk
www.LifesMeaningforToday.com

Photography and cover design Katharina Weber
diekat.wordpress.com

Introduction

London February 2012.

This book first appeared not in print but on the internet in the form of a daily quote for me to use for life's meaning for today. By meaning I refer to the fact that every day our life unfolds another aspect or element of True Self emerges if only we stop and take the time to recognise what it is that is being reflected back to us to show who we really are and another facet of our being.

In creating this book I have taken each of the various days 'life's meaning' as well as additional quotes from my book 'The Power of Caring and Your Field of Perception' making it possible to select a page at random and read a statement which reflects back an important element of your True Self in your life.

The question will emerge for many as they read this book 'how do I respond to the events as I see them from a new and different perspective?' My answer is to allow yourself time to reflect on what you are now experiencing from an expansive way of thinking about and relating to your daily waking life.

Enjoy using this short book at many levels as you make the necessary changes to step forward to the next unfolding stages of your future.

It is now over a year since the first edition of Life's Meaning for Today appeared and I wish to share a few thoughts and observations gained from my many readers.

I will admit that it came as a pleasant surprise when I was told of one gentleman, retired in his early nineties who consulted the book every morning on waking and like many people he would simply think of a question and then open a page at random. So many people have reported how, when they open a page at random, the statement or 'quote' exactly mirrors their thoughts, feelings or aspirations at that moment in time.

The response to Life's Meaning for Today has created untold ideas within me and on more than one occasion brought a broad smile to my face as readers told me of both their thoughts and related experiences on reading the first printing of my book.

Since the second publication, with additional material as quotes the idea of a journal where people could write their own thoughts and reflections came into being and so an accompanying 'Life's Meaning Journal' is now available.

As you read the various quotes for some there will be terms such as True Self, parallel life expressions and soul expression which you may not have encountered before. Or, perhaps, you have but in outline only.

So then not to confuse or misdirect your feeling as you read and respond let me explain how they are a part of my philosophy.

My philosophy came into being , was created or emerged from my career in working with the dying, the bereaved and people who were facing loss, transition and change in their lives or the lives of those around them.

Then early in 2001 I formulated Dynamic Cognition as an accessible model of understanding the complex, multifaceted exploration of our connection with True Self which I had shared with the many people I had worked with over the years. I chose the term Dynamic Cognition because thought and reflection through our conversation with True Self connects us with the multifaceted person we really are.

The question is whether we are consciously or remain consciously aware of these key elements which result from our connection with True Self. Note: You will notice that throughout the book of quotes there are no page numbers. This has been designed on purpose so that you manipulate the illusion of so called structure and reality composing our lives.

Steven Warren
London **28th February 2012**

With thanks

To all of those I have worked with in my thirty year career. You reflected your wisdom so I might discover and express my own wisdom.

It is with words you speak and communicate with your heart

but your mind is not receptive to your hearts words save for periods when circumstance dictates that your conscious mind should become quiet.

Commanding your own life takes courage.

The courage to realise and overcome the blocks we put in place to recognising how we are in control of our present and future life.

Other people and circumstances in the world outside ourselves

are put forward as the reasons for problems and obstacles to, what we really feel in our heart, the life we truly want.

The problem for most people is how they put their hearts desires last in life and so don't know how to communicate with their True Self.

In our modern world how often do we hear the hearts rule

being blamed for problems in a person's life when, in reality, our conscious mind made false promises that it didn't know how to keep.

Fear is something we create

when we don't fully understand either a situation or ourselves.

When we have gone against our true values be they honesty, truthfulness, clarity, to other people or ourselves then the only feeling is fear.

Our fear guides us to leave or make changes

so that we need never feel the fear of the situation we currently face ever again.

As an example, for many to fall in love creates fear but the time when they fell in love was not true love for true love is beyond fear, death and life itself.

Soul weary is when we have walked a path which doesn't fully represent who we really are.

It may be that we have moved into the next phase of our life and the world outside us hasn't appeared to catch up with the fundamental shift.

Or, and more importantly, it may be we haven't appeared to catch up with such a fundamental shift within ourselves and instead are holding on to the old, familiar and outdated ways of being.

Every person we will meet in our lives

no matter how marked our difference in race, culture, sex, age or beliefs, there will be one thing in life we agree upon.

For we all share one common purpose in life and how we interpret and live our life in the journey shows diversity, truth and above all meaning.

Playtime is our creative space to put in action the next stages of our lives.

Learning, understandings, feelings, thoughts all come from play.

To play with life results in our inner wisdom creating a truthful and therefore meaningful life.

Wisdom. Children create far greater wisdom

through simple honesty allowing access to our timeless, boundless wisdom within.

We all know and understand everything about our lives when the conscious chatter of the adult mind is calmed and made quiet.

Clearing our lives to engage in the next phase of our life is where we invite the adult self into our world.

The wise inner voice watches as the practical parts of life are changed around us.

Patience, more patience dispels the growing boredom and finally gives way to our boundless enthusiasm as we play out and explore our future.

Reflection upon what has gone before.

Reflection from others and who they see we are.

Reflection on the future we may or may not see from our present.

Reflections on our mind from our heart life reveal the multifaceted diamond our soul really is here, in the future from the past of our life.

Journeying through our lives provides diverse paths.

Some we appear to detour down with others and some journeys we explore with purposeful steps.

We mingle and match our pathways through life with many others. We knew of our purpose but are enlightened by the journey with all the twists and turns which we could never have imagined.

Such is the richness of every life lived no matter how short or long.

If in work we express what we achieve for ourselves and then for others

then expression is complete so we can fully receive from others. It is important to judge how far we have limited ourselves in order to break free of the bonds we have imposed upon ourselves.

Life in this world is full of limitless

expression,

understanding,

opportunities

and people to meet.

When we realise the expansion of our thoughts we may need to anchor our days and our days within weeks and our weeks within months.

Why - because to discover our limitless potential brings a time of being overwhelmed in our thinking and subsequent action.

It takes most of us time to adjust our daily action to contain our realisation of our real life.

Whose plan when synchronous events happen

to enfold the many lives of those we have met or yet to meet with events intertwined and yet to be known.

Our plan is to recognise that such a connection exists to unify us all at every level and in every way so a fuller life of many potentials may unfold.

All About Your Life

Have you asked questions in your life to find out who you can be?

You read, you ask, you listen.

Who am I how can I express what I know and feel?

I want to tell you about how you can live your life, how your life can be and then I'll ask you one question.

Which of your lives do you want to choose?

Think about it.

All About Your Life

The life that is half fulfilled or the one that is filled with all your aspirations of who you know how to be.

Your life, your destiny going forward and understanding all that you can be.

By finding a meaning in life and expressing it to the full.

Ideals and dreams and knowing what you can achieve.

Loving to the full following your passion.

Bringing life into full focus and expressing all you need.

Beginning now living all the life you have before you die.

Serenity Found

How by your inner knowing.

Being real.

Knowing what your life is and who you are now.

Who is this person and what do they say?

How do you express that which is within your heart?

When you find your voice empty of anger, empty of pain but full of love for who you really are.

Greet your heart and express, in what you say, how you are to those around you.

Honesty in how you listen to what their heart is telling you about them.

A life lived to the full requires the courage of your mind to trust your heart.

In trusting your heart with childish knowing even when those around never understand your wisdom.

For now to stay to leave?

To find another way?

Love is for who in your life and for how long?

The only person who will journey through your life, from beginning to end, is one special person - YOU.

To love you is to know you. To know you is to love you. How many times will we let people stand between the most important relationship in our life?

For this is my complete work

To witness another's understanding

To witness another's passion

To witness another's creativity

To witness another's love

To witness another

Do you agree how when we have a fulfilling relationship . .

with our True Self then all of the relationships we have or are yet to make take on a new light. How do you see them illuminated from such a new light?

Inspiration is around us every waking day of our lives.

It never changes or comes and goes. No, it is rather we who fluctuate between being connected as we create or act to remove blocks to the flow of such inspiration in our daily lives.

A phone call today, a message of invitation.

To be surprised by life is one of the most precious joys which can be taken as a gift.

What and who is a thing of our past and how we relate to our future?

The people and places from our past are no longer a part of us save in our dreams and they exist as dreams to enable us to mould a different future.

To travel far in our lives is a journey which began before we were born.

Our birth was to engage on such a journey and never will we falter with each step we take throughout life.

To embark on expressing our wisdom

as images and not words which tumble in a myriad of expressions requires the mirror of another to enable our wisdom to come forth.

To support another,

To,

Express their creativity

Express their passion

Express their unique knowing

Express their care

Express their understanding

Perspectives change as our life unfolds

bringing new ideas, experiences, understanding, loss and gain. True perspective is wider and larger than our life and each day's events for us are within but not of this world.

Understanding and wisdom of life are our birthright

which some handle with care for the precious self we are.

When our life may appear broken we may look within and discover the depth of our wise understanding of the event which has unfolded.

The reflections of our futures are often seen from our past

but not of our own thoughts but rather what others saw and reflected to us then.

Examine what they saw and told you now in your present and from this you will know your future.

How can you know and enjoy the light unless you see the darkness.

Not all will know or understand what we know, see and understand but such people are there for us as much as we might be there for them.

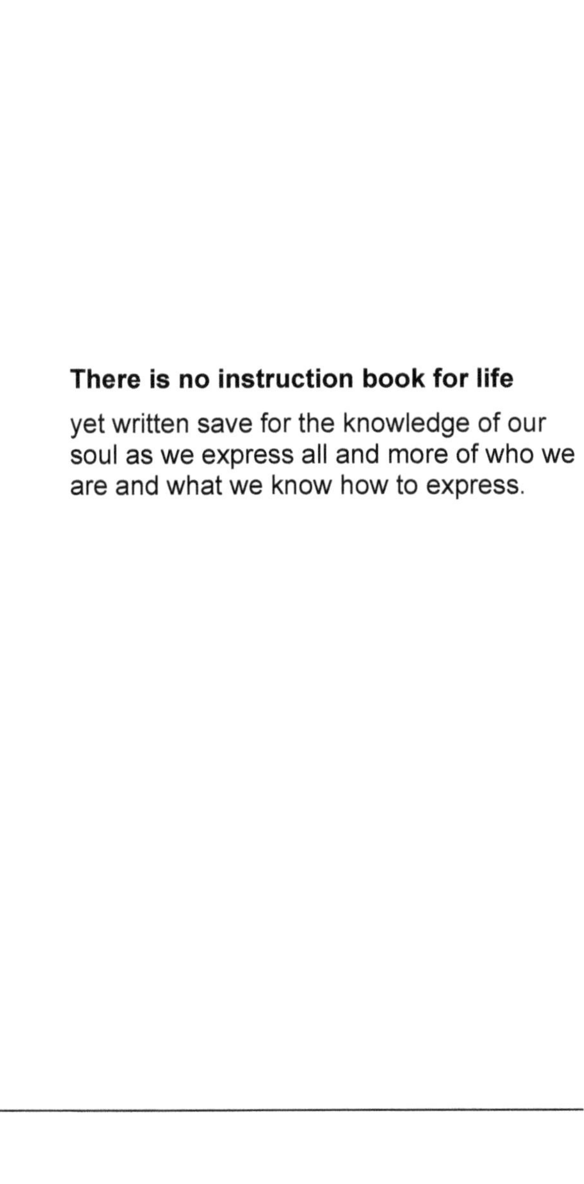

There is no instruction book for life

yet written save for the knowledge of our soul as we express all and more of who we are and what we know how to express.

To play is to work and to work is to play.

To play is to create, to work is to create.

To love is to create

To love is to exchange and in such exchange consciously discover and to see another part of my true being and witness such expression

If you find me as I wait for you then stand close so I may know you

If you find me when I am lost in life then hold me close until I am sure again

If you find me when I am no longer with you here in this life then hold me close until you are sure again

If I find you then our hearts will know

If you find me make me yours so I may be sure we are real

If you find me then I shall stand with you in life through the passing days till we meet again on another shore

Of all my tomorrows

Tomorrows known and unknown

Tomorrows real and imagined

Tomorrows I will believe in from my heart

Tomorrows I shall discard with my mind

Loves I shall know

Loves I shall borrow

Loves I shall cherish

Loves which I shall once more discover in THIS LIFE

Soul mates do not exist

but are instead soul connections or reflections with such a connection spanning many parallel lives to enrich and explore the various facets which compose this and each of the parallel lives we share our soul connections within.

Karma does not exist

for there is no time and all our individual parallel life expressions are lived as one

……

When I know myself

Why then I shall see another

A real me

When I see the real me

Why then I shall see another

Those who compose

The diamond

expression of my soul.

To return to a theme in our life

brings a simple lesson into sharp focus. What one simple thing do we need to change in this regard - forever?

To lose track of time is to liberate one aspect of self beyond measure.

Then to return to time with such insight means you know where you really are.

Power resides within oneself.

We may share our thoughts, feelings, life and journey but only when we choose to do so.

How often we forget how the choice is always ours.

Transitions,

how many and in how many ways to have known, discovered, celebrated in your life and how would you tell another of the joy which resides in your heart in living such a life?

Soul weary

is when we have walked a path which doesn't fully represent who we really are.

We resonate from our past but from a distance

which is a firm and a clear place of strength, power and choice for our future. In viewing and choosing our past the future becomes clear and honest.

As we enter each season of our lives

we bathe in the warmth of our summers gone, autumns of reflection and springs of revelation which bring forth the multifaceted layers of our unique being.

We all know how to love

but as time passes we learn the nature of how to engage in both the love from others and equally our love for ourselves.

In ageing we grow closer to the self we left in our childhood

as we no longer look to the outside world but to our inner self to know both who we really are and why we are here.

A reflection of the future is closer than we often realise.

To know is the simple action of quietening our conscious mind for even a short while in time and then seeing our dreams as our reality.

As another year moves towards our personal history

we reflect no longer on the past but celebrate what has been and who we really are along the journey we wish to call our life.

What answers echo in our mind?

To remain

When other's have gone
Is simply a place in time
But where is time
Where are we and
Where are they?

You created this life full of purpose

to blend with other lives from your parallel life expressions to reflect True Self to every person you shall meet and in doing so understand every event you will experience for you are not here to learn anything but to express all you knew before this life.

The many unions in our lives,

be they with friends, with our family, with the many facets of self is the pleasure which composes the day of this particular earthly life and the many lives we share beyond this one life.

To know our soul expression is to know ourselves

and then to revel in the power we wait yet to express.

We inspire others as we take our breath away

when we speak our truth.

A truth as old as time which can be heard by all who care enough to listen.

When we cannot see our direction

then we know our real goal

and when we are lost we begin the real journey

I stand with me like no other I have known

I stand with me alone

I stand me with me knowing clearly

I stand with me embracing a life

My life

I stand with me

Call forth no one other

than yourself and express who you truly are

so others may receive and thereby respond in truth.

Nothing other than that which you know from your heart as instruction for your mind.

Allow life to be lived as experience of a greater knowing which observes life's path in all its expression.

Pleasure becomes us

As satisfaction grows
From each expression
Each encounter
Which unfolds within
The hours of our days

To be without conscience is to disconnect from our soul.

To be only conscious is to disconnect from our heart.

To be so asleep in our lives is to experience living death.

Often, without knowing,

we witness our lives from afar and in such awareness we know the real truth of our life.

In the support of those who have gone before

to inspire, to go within and find the strength to follow and to smile and find our voice then we shall speak our truth so that we may see our future with clarity.

How might we know our heart if it were not for sharing in the love of others

and in such sharing building a bridge between our lives to cover our aloneness.

Only when we share love will we never know loneliness, isolation, separation ever again in this life.

The life I knew

The life I dreamt of
The life I imagined
The life I made
The life I care for
The life I respect
The life I love
The life I keep
Close to my heart
The life I share
The life I remember
The life I see
Which mirrors all lives
Known and unknown
Seen and witnessed
Expressed to the full.

How will we know when life speaks to us?

When we are shown by those around us and the events we create. In such creation we witness our expression as a soulful being in this our life.

When we witness this with our heart then our mind knows the breadth of our true being.

We then know that we are real and alive within this our life.

Not by that which we may own.

Not by that which we can buy.

No, we know that we are alive within this our life through the people who share our love.

When we cannot see our direction
then we know our real goal
and when we are lost
we begin the real journey.

Of all my tomorrows

Tomorrows known and unknown

Tomorrows real and imagined

Tomorrows I will believe in from my heart

Tomorrows I shall discard with my mind

Loves I shall know

Loves I shall borrow

Loves I shall cherish

Loves which I shall once more discover in THIS LIFE.

To know our soul expression is to know ourselves

and then to revel in the power we wait yet to express.

To keep focus on the reality of now

is to draw past knowing and understand what the now reflects back to us so we step into our real future.

How often do we create time to celebrate our past?

All the love, the loss, the gain, the journey of growing towards unfolding

this life which we created.

Humanness is full of emotions

such as pain, joy, fear, courage, achievement and finally, wonderment.

No matter what age we might be we still have our breath taken away at the wonder of the world we live in.

The Three C's

Empowerment arises from the three Cs:

Choice,
Courage and
Change.

They are yours to claim

.

What are the real dreams

which reflect the real you rather than borrowed aspirations

from those in the world around you?

When we aren't fully real we explore one important aspect of life

not knowing

and on the voyage of discovery others reflect back who we really are.

We listen, we learn, we love, we share in relationships which are either complete or incomplete, careers which are true or false

through a sea of life transitions towards discovering our own personal road map of clarity.

When you feel like running in life consider this:

is it always away from where you are or towards who you really are and what you really want in this life?

Publications and Recordings

Life's Meaning JOURNAL

Steven Warren

The quotes written by Steven Warren which are included in this journal are taken from the second edition of Life's Meaning for Today.

Enjoy using this journal at many levels as you make the necessary changes to step forward to the next unfolding stages of your future life. www.LifesMeaningForToday.com

ISBN 978-1-908587-02-2

Dynamic Cognition – The DC Effect in Your Life

Steven Warren

This aspect of Steven Warren's philosophy was created in 2003 and has been at the basis of his work, both writing and talks, for nine years. Besides detailing the philosophy of the DC Effect Steven examines common examples of Dynamic Cognition resulting from a sustained connection with True Self in our day-to-day life.

In Press. Publication 2012
www.dceffect.com

Life's Meaning for Today Audio Recording

At the same time as the second edition of this popular book of quotes for Life's Meaning Steven has recorded an audio version which can be downloaded from these websites:
www.StevenWarren.co.uk
www.LifesMeaningForToday.com

NEWSLETTER SUBSCRIPTION
If you would like to receive regular up-dates then please send an email to
news@StevenWarren.co.uk

www.ingramcontent.com/pod-product-compliance
Ingram Content Group UK Ltd.
Pitfield, Milton Keynes, MK11 3LW, UK
UKHW020222250726
13967UKWH00001B/145

9 781908 587015